OUR DIGITAL PLANET

How Coding Works

by Ben Hubbard

capstone

E
005.1
HUB

To contact Capstone Global Library please phone 800-747-4992, or visit our website www.mycapstone.com

Edited by Nikki Potts
Designed by Sarah Bennett
Picture research by Ruth Smith
Production by Laura Manthe
Originated by Capstone Global Library Limited
Printed and bound in China
007875

Library of Congress Cataloging-in-Publication Data
Names: Hubbard, Ben, 1973--author.
Title: How coding works / by Ben Hubbard.
Description: North Mankato, Minnesota : Heinemann Raintree, a Capstone imprint, [2017] | Series: Heinemann read and learn. Our digital planet | Audience: Ages 6–8. | Audience: K to grade 3. | Includes bibliographical references and index.
Identifiers: LCCN 2016029367| ISBN 9781484635995 (library binding) | ISBN 9781484636039 (paperback) | ISBN 9781484636152 (ebook (pdf))
Subjects: LCSH: Computer programming—Juvenile literature.
Classification: LCC QA76.52 H82 2017 | DDC 005.1—dc23
LC record available at https://lccn.loc.gov/2016029367

Acknowledgements
We would like to thank the following for permission to reproduce photographs: Getty Images: Bloomberg, 12, 13; iStockphoto: DragonImages, 10, back cover left; Shutterstock: Angela Waye, 22 (surfing), Jason Winter, 9, Levent Konuk, 15, 22 (diagram), Monkey Business Images, 21, 22 (instruction), Nikolaeva, cover design element, interior design element, OlegDoroshin, 7, Ollyy, 8, photovibes, 5, ProStockStudio, cover, Rawpixel.com, 4, 6, 11, 18, 19, 22 (algorithm), (programmer), back cover right, studio0411, 14, Thongchai Kitiyanantawong, 17, wavebreakmedia, 20, 22 (task), welcomia, 16

We would like to thank Matt Anniss for his invaluable help in the preparation of this book.

Contents

Some words are shown in bold, **like this**.
You can find them in the glossary on page 22.

How Do Computers Work?

Computers can do many complicated things. They follow **instructions** to complete **tasks**.

Computers only do what they are told.
People provide the instructions.

What Are Programs?

A program is a set of **instructions** that a computer follows. Computers need programs for every **task** they do.

Programs allow us to **surf** the Internet, learn new things, or even play games. Computers could not do anything without programs.

What Is Code?

Computer programs are written in code. A computer's basic language is called "machine code."

Machine code is a series of the numbers "0" and "1." It is a language you can learn like any other.

What Is Coding?

Giving a computer a set of step-by-step **instructions** is called "coding."

Programmers write a set of instructions in code that humans can understand. The computer then turns these instructions into machine code.

What Is Coding Like?

Coding tells a computer what to do. These **instructions** can be as simple as "wait 5 seconds" and "play sound."

Computers only do what they are told. They cannot think for themselves.

What Is an Algorithm?

An **algorithm** is a list of coding steps for a computer program. Coding steps must be in the correct order for a program to work.

Programmers often draw a **diagram** of their algorithm. This helps them make sure the steps are in order.

What Are Some Coding Languages?

There are many coding languages. Each one is used to create different types of programs.

Games and websites are types of programs. Some common coding languages are Scratch, Python, Java, C, PHP, and Javascript.

How Are Coding Languages Different?

Each coding language has its own rules. The rules say which words and numbers should be used in a code language.

Programs will not work if the wrong words or numbers are used. Code can look strange at first. But many coding languages are easy to learn.

How Do I Become a Programmer?

There are many ways to become a **programmer**. Your school or community center may teach coding classes. You can also learn from books and the Internet.

Ask an adult to help you try the coding websites found at the link on page 23.

Glossary

 **algorithm** a list of steps a programmer gives a computer to perform a task or solve a problem

 **diagram** simple drawing that shows how something works

 **instruction** command or order telling something or someone to do something

 **programmer** person who writes computer programs

 **surfing** moving from website to website on the Internet to look for something

 **task** piece of work to be done

Find Out More

Books

Lyons, Heather. *A World of Programming.* Kids Get Coding. Minneapolis: Lerner Publications, 2017.

Vorderman, Carol. *Help Your Kids With Computer Coding: A Unique Step-by-Step Visual Guide, From Binary Code to Building Games.* Computer Programming. New York: DK Publishing, 2014.

Yearling, Tricia. *How Do I Play Games Online.* Online Smarts. New York: Enslow Publishing, 2015.

Internet Sites

Facthound offers a safe, fun way to find Internet sites related to this book. All of the sites on Facthound have been researched by our staff.

Here's all you do:
Visit *www.facthound.com*
Type in this code: 9781484635995

Index